life
underground

Translation: Jean Grasso Fitzpatrick

©Parramón Ediciones, S.A.
First Edition, October, 1986
The title of the Spanish edition is *la vida bajo la tierra*

All inquiries should be addressed to:
Barron's Educational Series, Inc.
250 Wireless Boulevard
Hauppauge, New York 11788

Library of Congress Catalog Card No. 87-12546

International Standard Book No. 0-8120-3862-2

Library of Congress Cataloging-in-Publication Data
Rius, María.
    Life underground

    (Habitats)
    Translation of: La vida bajo la tierra.
    Summary: Papa Bunny explains to his little bunny
rabbit how their underground home was built by digging
through various layers of earth.
    [1. Rabbits — Fiction. 2. Animals — Habitations —
Fiction] I. Parramón, José María.   II. Title.
III. Series: Rius, María. Habitats.
PZ7.R5213Lm   1987   [E]   87-12546
ISBN 0-8120-3862-2

Legal Deposit: B-41.000-87

Printed in Spain by Cayfosa
Sta. Perpètua de Mogoda
(Barcelona)

7 8 9   9960   9 8 7 6 5 4 3 2

habitats

life underground

María Rius
J. M. Parramón

BARRON'S

New York • Toronto • Sydney

Once upon a time there was a little bunny rabbit...

... who lived in the woods and ran and jumped and played with Papa Bunny and Mama Bunny.

"Papa Bunny knows everything," said the little bunny rabbit. "One day he said to me, 'Do you see the carrots and the grass? You may eat them, but you must never eat flowers, or mushrooms, or snails.'"

"The next day he said to me, 'Do you see those children? You can play with them, because they're nice and small, just like you.'"

"The next day he told me, 'But if you ever see men with a dog and guns, run home as fast as you can! Those are rabbit hunters!' "

"Do you see my home? I live in a hole that's too deep and too narrow for dogs or hunters to get in," said the little bunny rabbit.

"When Papa Bunny and Mama Bunny began to dig my home ...

… first they found the small roots of plants and wildflowers, then soil, then a layer of rocks…

Then they got to a layer of sand, and the roots of a huge tree, and the root of a plant that looked like an onion. . . .

Further along they ran into another tunnel! It belonged to a mole – another animal that lives underground....

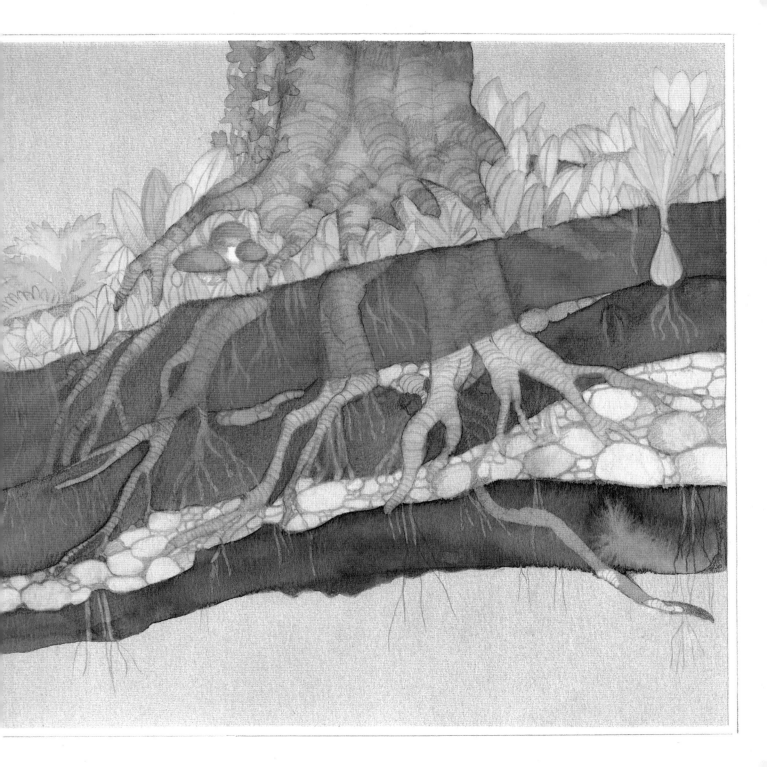

And then they found worms and roots, and potatoes, and ants digging in the soil....

Until at last they finished, and the house was ready."

"This is the place where my brother and sister bunny rabbits and I were born. In our home it's never too cold or too hot, and it never rains or snows. Papa Bunny brings us food when the hunting dogs are in the woods. We're all happy here! THIS IS LIFE UNDERGROUND!"

LIFE UNDERGROUND

The ground looks perfectly still, but under it is a busy, fertile world of animal and plant life.

Is there life underground?

Sometimes it seems as though most living things live *on* the land, but that's not true. Just take a look at a few layers of earth, and you will see another world, with its own biological rhythm, many tiny animals, and seeds from which plants grow.

Rabbits and holes

Some animals — like the rabbit and the mole — dig long tunnels underground and make holes or burrows to live in at the end.

There they are far away from hot and cold weather. They don't have to worry about being attacked by other animals or by people, and they feel safe.

The rabbit is one of the most useful animals. Rabbits can be raised on farms, although they also live in the wild. They eat grass and herbs. In fact, some people like to eat rabbit meat because it tastes like rosemary and thyme. The rabbit is one of the most fertile animals. Each female rabbit can have several litters a year; in each litter are six or seven little rabbits! The mother rabbit feeds her babies with her milk. Some people also like rabbit fur. It is used to make warm linings for gloves and boots.

Mining and wells

By digging mines and wells in the ground, people find many useful things. We get oil and water from wells, and coal, silver, gold, and diamonds from mines.

How seeds grow

Not only ants and worms live underground; there are also seeds from which plants grow. Seeds may take root themselves or may be planted by the farmer. They take in oxygen and water. Before long, they sprout stems that grow up above the ground and roots that anchor the plant and help it get water and food from the soil.